Science World

General editors · David & Simon Joll

Anna Sproule

Food for the World

The right of the
University of Cambridge
to print and sell
all manner of books
was granted by
Henry VIII in 1534.
The University has printed
and published continuously
since 1584.

CAMBRIDGE UNIVERSITY PRESS

Cambridge · London · New York · New Rochelle · Melbourne · Sydney

Contents

NOTE TO THE READER: while you are reading this book you will notice that certain words appear in **bold type**. This is to indicate a word listed in the Glossary on page 45. This glossary gives brief explanations of words which may be new to you.

Acknowlegements

The Publishers wish to thank the following organizations for their invaluable assistance in the preparation of this book.

ICI — Plant protection
Japan National Tourist Organization
Oxfam
Safeway Foodstores

Photographic credits

t = top   b = bottom   l = left   r = right   c = centre

5 Peter Stevenson/Seaphot; 6, 8, 9*t*, 9*b* The Hutchison Library; 11, 13*t*, 13*b*, 14 ZEFA; 15 John Lythgoe/Seaphot; 16 ZEFA; 17 The Hutchison Library; 18 ICI Plant Protection; 19 John Lythgoe/Seaphot; 20, 25*t*, 25*b*, 26*b* The Hutchison Library; 26*t* ZEFA; 27 The Hutchison Library; 28*t*, 28*b* John Lythgoe/Seaphot; 31*t* Japan National Tourist Organization; 31*b* South American Pictures; 32 Safeway Foodstores; 33, 35 ZEFA; 40 Oxfam; 41*t*, 41*b* The Hutchison Library; 42*l* ICI — Plant Protection; 42*r*, 44 ZEFA

Illustrations by David Anstey, Peter Endsleigh Castle, Sallie Alane Reason

Published by the
Press Syndicate of the University of Cambridge
The Pitt Building, Trumpington Street, Cambridge CB2 1RP
32 East 57th Street, New York, NY 10022, USA
10 Stamford Road, Oakleigh, Melbourne 3166, Australia

© BLA Publishing Limited 1987

First published 1987

British Library cataloguing in publication data

Sproule, Anna
   Food for the world. — (Science world).
   1. Food — Juvenile literature
   I. Title   II. Series
   641.3   TX355

ISBN 0-521-33240-0

Designed and produced by BLA Publishing Limited, Swan Court, East Grinstead, Sussex, England.

A member of the **Ling Kee Group**
LONDON · HONG KONG · TAIPEI · SINGAPORE · NEW YORK

Colour origination by Waterden Reproductions Limited
Printed in Italy by New Interlitho

Food for the world

We all need food. Without it, we could not live. Animals and plants need food as well. For plants, animals and people, food is one of the most important things in the world.

In a rich country, having enough to eat is easy. People buy most of their food from stores and supermarkets. If their supplies run low, they can easily go out and buy more.

In poor countries, many people grow their own food. Some years their crops are good. Then each family has enough to eat. If the crops are bad, then some families go hungry. They cannot buy extra food because they do not have enough money.

Food and farming

Different foods grow best in different **climates**. Sugar cane grows in lands which have hot climates. Potatoes grow well in cool lands. Fruits like peaches and grapes need plenty of sun to help them become ripe.

Some types of land are better than others for growing food. Land that is very dry or wet, or that slopes very steeply, is hard to farm. Farmers are always trying to grow better crops. Scientists often help the farmers. Together, they are working out ways of growing more food to feed the world.

▼ Where large crops of wheat are grown, the grain is often stored in huge buildings called silos.

What is food?

If a car runs out of fuel, it stops. If an animal runs out of food, it starves. Food is the fuel which keeps our bodies going. It gives us the **energy** we need to stay alive. We all need water too.

We need to eat often because we are always using up energy. Our hearts need energy to keep beating. Our lungs need it to keep breathing. So, even when we stand still we are using energy. Running uses a lot more. Food replaces all the energy we use up.

The boxes below compare the amount of food people need at different ages, compared with their weights. Men and women doing the same kind of work need the same amount of food.

What is food made of?

Our bodies use food to give us energy. We use food in other ways, as well. Food helps the body to grow. It helps the body to make strong teeth and bones. It also keeps the body warm. The things in food that do all these jobs are called **nutrients**.

There are five different types of nutrient in food. One nutrient is called **protein**. This is what makes the body grow. It also helps the body replace old or damaged parts. **Fat** is another nutrient. It gives the body a lot of energy. A layer of fat under the skin also helps to keep the cold out. Nutrients called **carbohydrates** also supply the body with energy.

Vitamins are the fourth type of nutrient. There are many vitamins and we all need tiny amounts of each. If we do not have them, our bodies do not work well. **Minerals** also help the body to grow and work well.

Different foods

Many foods have several types of nutrient in them. Some have only one. There is no single kind of food which contains all the nutrients we need. This means that we must eat a mixture of foods to stay healthy. A good mixture, or balanced **diet**, gives the body everything it needs. Meat gives us protein. So do eggs, fish and milk. Meat, milk, egg yolks and some fish also give us fat. Foods like bread, honey and pasta give us carbohydrates.

Take care to eat a mixture of foods. In the past, sailors on long sea voyages often became ill. Their bodies hurt and their teeth fell out. Sometimes they died. They became ill because they were not eating any fresh fruit. Fruits contain important vitamins that keep our bodies healthy.

Diets around the world

People around the world eat many types of food to give them all they need. Often they use the foods that grow well in their own countries. Some people have strict rules about what to eat. **Vegetarians**, for example, do not eat any meat.

In Japan, many people have boiled rice and raw eggs for breakfast. In Europe, many people have fried eggs on bread. These breakfasts sound different, but they are both balanced meals. Rice and bread both contain carbohydrates. The eggs have protein.

Some national foods

Rice and bread are both **staple foods**. A staple food is the most important part of a diet. Rice is the staple food of many countries in the Far East. Bread is important in America and Europe. It is usually made out of wheat.

▲ These monks from Thailand are vegetarians. They do not eat any meat.

Oats are another type of staple food. Oats like cool, damp climates. They can be made into cakes. In Italy, corn meal is used to make a porridge called 'polenta'. People in Mexico use corn meal to make pancakes called 'tortillas'. In India, they eat a flat bread made from wheat, called 'chapatti'.

People eat many different types of meat as well. In China, they like pork. In the Middle East, lamb and chicken are eaten. The religious beliefs of the Jews and Muslims stop them from eating pork.

In India, Hindu people believe that cows are holy. Because of this, they do not eat beef. They do not eat pork either, and many do not eat meat at all.

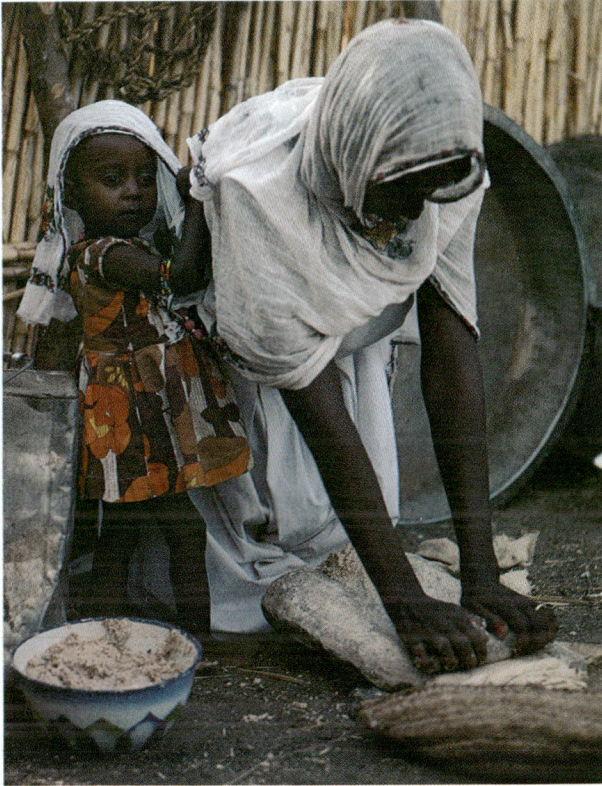

Food for all

Some countries in the world are very rich. They grow lots of food. They sell what their people do not eat. Others are very poor. They cannot grow enough food, and they are too poor to buy from the richer ones.

Scientists try to help the farmers in poor countries. One way is to grow crops which give better **yields**. They also help the farmers to make better use of their land and climate.

There are about 500 million people in the world who do not get enough to eat. Most of them live in poor countries where it is often difficult to grow enough food.

◀ The African woman is making bread from a crop called sorghum.

▼ These farmers are working on a crop-growing project in Africa. They are trying to make the best use of their land.

Food for plants

Plants, like people, need food to keep them alive and help them grow. They also need water. Water is very important.

Plants, unlike people, can make their own food. To make their food, plants use the energy which is in sunlight.

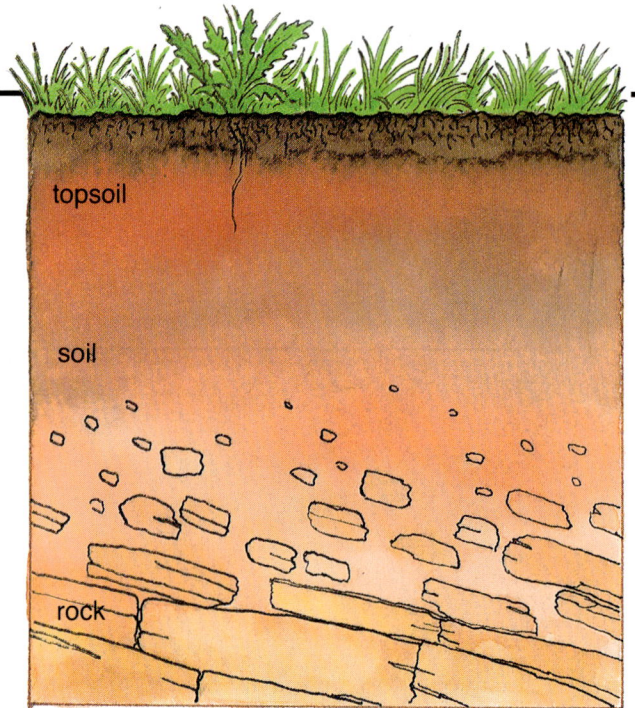

sunlight
water
carbon dioxide

topsoil

soil

rock

How plants make food

A plant makes its food in its leaves. To make the food, a plant needs water, sunlight, and a gas in the air called **carbon dioxide**. The roots of the plant take up the water from the soil. The leaves take in the gas from the air. They also catch the sunlight. The leaves are able to do this because they contain a green **chemical** called **chlorophyll**. The chemical soaks up the light which shines on the leaves.

Plants use the sunlight's energy, water and carbon dioxide to make a sugary food. Making food like this is called **photosynthesis**. When this takes place, plants make another gas called **oxygen**. Plants make more oxygen than they need. They give some of the oxygen out into the air. Animals use this oxygen to breathe. Most of the world's oxygen comes from plants. Can you think what would happen without it?

Food from the soil

The soil a plant grows in contains things called minerals. Some of these minerals are needed by plants. One of them is called magnesium. Plants use this to make chlorophyll. Another is nitrogen. This is very important, because plants use it to make protein. This makes plants grow leafy and big.

When plants and animals die, their remains rot into the ground. The minerals they contain go back to the soil and make it richer. This helps new plants to grow.

▼ Very few types of plant grow in deserts because there is so little rain.

Where plants grow

There are many places where plants do not grow well. Only one tenth of the world's land is really good for growing crops. The lands near the North and South Poles, for example, are too cold. The deserts are too dry. A big area of desert stretches right across the north of Africa and the Middle East. Many of the countries in this large area cannot grow much food.

Rich countries often have land where plenty of crops can be grown. The richest is the USA. The US farmers can grow four times as much from their land as the farmers in Africa.

Plants for food

In most parts of the world, people's main food comes from plants. Many of these plants are types of grass, which we call **cereals**. We eat the **seeds** of these plants.

Growing the crops

In Europe, wheat is sown in the autumn. It grows its tall stems the next year. In America, a lot of wheat is not sown until the spring. It is cut later in the year than the other type.

Wheat and most other cereals are grown in normal fields. But rice needs a lot of water. Rice farmers make fields like big ponds, called paddy fields. They are filled with water while the rice grows. Then they are drained before the **harvest**. In Africa, crops like maize are planted just before the rains begin.

Harvesting

Farmers watch their crops closely as they grow. When the seeds are ripe, the crop is ready for harvesting. The farmer harvests the crop before the seeds scatter. Wheat is harvested by **combine harvesters**. These large machines do several jobs at once. They cut the stems, take out the grain and transfer it to trucks.

Rice can be harvested by machine or by hand. The dry paddies can then be used for other crops.

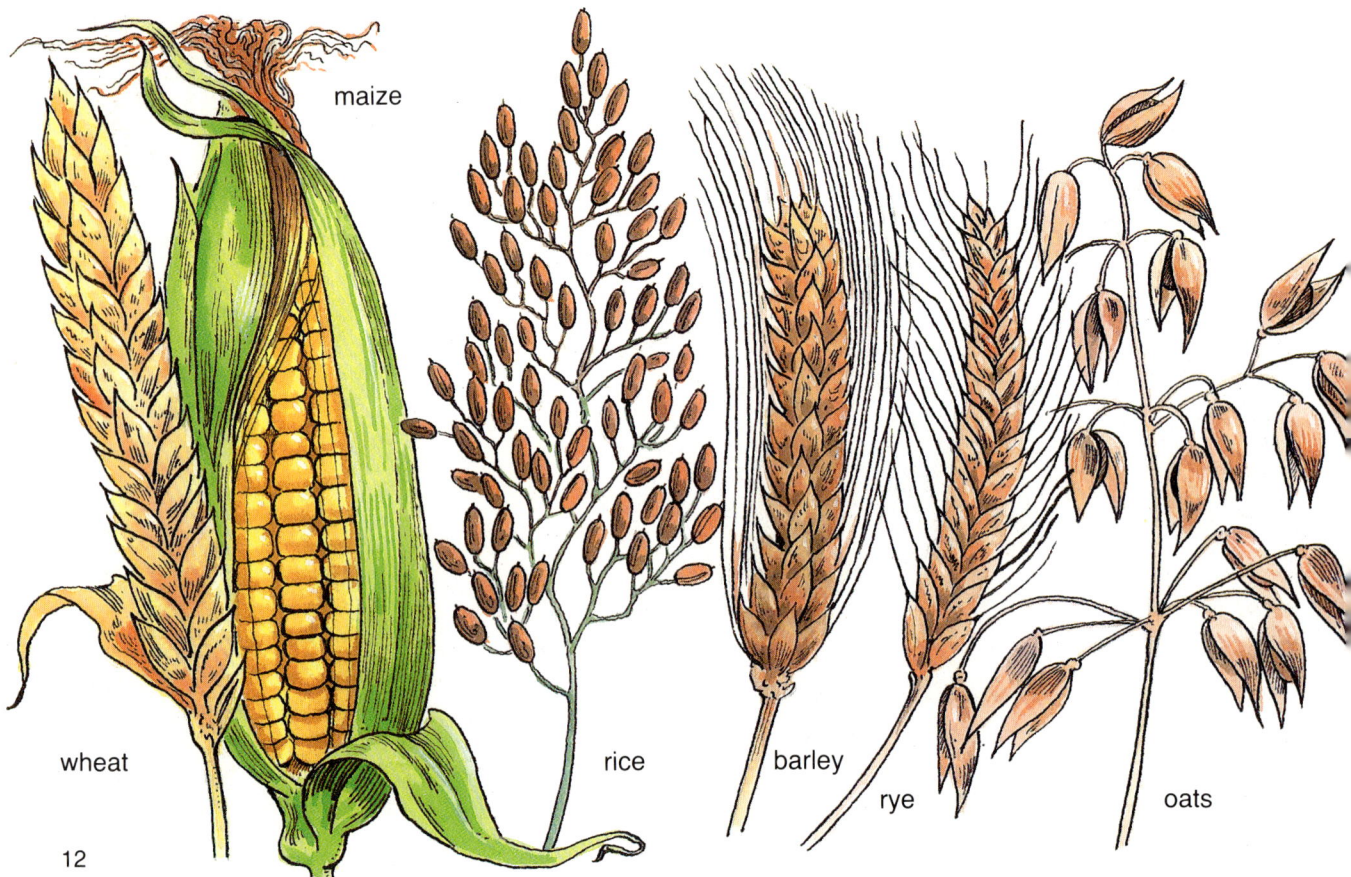

maize

wheat

rice

barley

rye

oats

▲ Young rice plants need plenty of water. They are planted in paddy fields.

▲ Cattle and other animals can eat grass, but we cannot do so. We eat the seeds of grasses. These are called cereals.

There are six main types of cereal. Wheat is grown in North and South America, Europe and India. Maize (called corn in America) is grown in America, Europe and Africa. Rice is a staple food in China, Japan and India. Oats and rye grow well in northern Europe. Barley is often grown for feeding cattle, but in parts of Asia it is one of the main human foods.

Grain for the world

In some countries, farmers grow grain to make money. They do not eat their own crops. They sell them. Often their crops go to people in other parts of the world.

In other countries, many people cannot grow enough grain. They are too poor to buy much from abroad. The people go hungry, even though there is grain for sale in the rich countries.

Vegetables we eat

We grow cereal crops for their seeds. The seeds of some plants we eat are so small we hardly notice them. The strawberry pips that catch between your teeth contain the tiny seeds!

We grow strawberries for the soft covering round their seeds. Pears, plums and peaches also have soft coverings. They are all fruits.

Seeds and fruits are not the only parts of plants we eat. We also eat the stems, leaves and roots of some plants. Celery is a stem. Cabbages and lettuces are made up of leaves. Carrots are roots. All these foods are **vegetables**.

▶ Believe it or not, a potato is not a root vegetable. Each potato is really a piece of plant stem.

Roots and bulbs

The roots of a plant hold it firmly in the ground. They also take in water and minerals from the soil. The roots of some plants swell up to make food stores, called **tubers**.

Other types of underground food stores are called bulbs. Most bulbs, like onions, are round in shape and made up of many layers. Most of the underground food stores which we eat are called **root crops**.

Most roots store a food called **starch**. Starch gives us plenty of energy. In some roots, the starch has been turned into sugar. Beetroot and sugar beet contain sugar. Sugar beet is not grown as a vegetable to eat. The crop is chopped up and soaked to get the sugar out.

▼ **This machine is harvesting sugar beet.**

pea

soya

Leaves and seeds

Root crops are often brown, yellow or red. Most of the green vegetables we eat are leaves and stems. One or two are flowers. The white part of a cauliflower is a collection of small flowers.

Seeds like peas and beans are important foods in many parts of the world. When dried, these sorts of seeds are called **pulses**. Pulses are rich in nutrients. Soya beans contain a lot of protein. They are often used instead of meat in vegetarian diets.

Many green vegetables have to be eaten soon after they are harvested. Root vegetables can be kept for some time if they are stored in a cool, dark place. Vegetables like beans and peas are dried and then kept for a long time. Dried beans and peas can be eaten all through the year.

Where is fruit grown?

Most of us think of fruit as something fresh, sweet and juicy. In fact, all plants have fruit. Peas, tomatoes and cucumbers are also fruit. 'Fruit' is the name given to the part of a plant which surrounds the seeds. The ears of grain are fruits, but we would not expect to see them in a fruit bowl.

Growing fruit

The crops we eat as fruit come from many parts of the world. In cool, temperate climates, fruits like apples and pears are grown. Soft fruits, like raspberries and stone fruits, like plums, are also grown. In warm countries, citrus fruits like oranges and lemons are grown.

Some fruits need very warm climates. They grow in the tropics. Mangoes and bananas are tropical fruits. Bananas are an important crop in Caribbean countries and South America. They grow in huge bunches. They have to be harvested by hand. The growers harvest them before they are ripe.

▼ A pineapple farm in Hawaii. The young plants have to be watered in the dry season. They need a lot of water to grow good fruit.

To the shops

Bananas often have a long journey to make before they reach the shops. That is why they are picked when they are green. They ripen on the long journeys.

Fruit travels to the shops from all over the world. A fruit bowl may hold fruit from six or seven countries. Some will have travelled thousands of kilometres. Others may have come from a farm nearby.

Some fruits are difficult to carry, or **transport**. They have to be kept fresh, so they have to travel quickly. Today, quick transport makes sure we enjoy fruit at its best. This was not the case a hundred years ago.

A lot of fruit goes by lorry. Some lorries have refrigerators in them. They stop the fruit from going bad. Some soft fruits are transported by air. This is costly, but the people who eat them do not mind paying the high prices. You can often tell which fruits have travelled by air. Just look at their prices in the shops!

▼ These ripe bananas have just been unloaded from a boat. They will need to be sold quickly.

Sprays and fertilizers

▲ The leaves from trees rot down. The nutrients in them are washed into the soil. They make more food for the trees.

As plants grow, they take nutrients from the earth. When the plants die, their leaves and stems fall to the ground and rot. The nutrients in them go back to the earth.

This does not always happen when plants are grown for food. When the crop is harvested, the goodness is taken away. The soil becomes less rich, or **fertile**. Because the soil contains less food, the next crop does not grow so well. Extra food, or **fertilizer**, has to be put into the soil by the farmer.

Food for the soil

There are two main types of fertilizer. **Organic** fertilizers come from the remains of plants and animals. Animal waste, or manure, is also organic. So is wood ash. Farmers also use 'green manure'. This is a crop which is grown and then dug back into the soil. It helps to feed the soil.

Chemical fertilizers are the other main types of fertilizer. They are made up of mixtures of chemicals. Different types of mixtures can be made, depending on the needs of each crop. The making of chemical fertilizers is a big industry.

▼ Can you see which lot of barley has been fed with fertilizer in this picture?

▲ Liquid manure is being sprayed on to the land to make the land more fertile.

Farmers have many ways of adding fertilizer to the soil. Just planting a crop like clover is one way. Manure is spread by a muck spreader. Chemical fertilizers are often powders or liquids. They are mixed up as sprays.

Crop diseases

If crops do not have the right food, they will become diseased. Some plants do not get enough iron from the soil. Their leaves start to turn yellow.

Diseases are also caused by types of **fungus**. One type of fungus harms the roots of cabbages. Another makes peach leaves go red and curl up. One deadly fungus kills potato plants. Fungi can be killed by sprays and powders.

Animal pests

A lot of harm is done to plants by animal pests. Birds eat the buds of fruit trees. Rabbits and other animals feed on the leaves of growing crops. Insects also feed on leaves. Some burrowing animals eat the roots of crops.

Farmers can protect crops by killing pests with poison. Some poisons are a danger to all life. The farmers have to be very careful which poisons they use.

19

Farm machines

In rich countries, most jobs on a farm can be done by machines. Some machines help in the fields. Others help in the farmyard, or in the farm office. The machines all help to reduce the need for human work. On some farms there are more machines than people.

On farms in poor countries, there are more people than machines. Much of the work is done by hand. Animals are used to help with the heavy work.

Machines help farmers grow much more food, but they are often expensive.

▼ The old and the new in India. Oxen are being used to draw a modern farm machine.

The tractor

The farmer's most useful machine is the tractor. In the past, horses and oxen helped farmers to plough the fields. They also helped with the harvests. They pulled ploughs and carts. This work is now done by tractors. Tractors pull other machines, like drills. A drill is the piece of farm equipment that sows the seeds.

A tractor is more than just a towing machine. It can be used to give its own power to other machines. These include hedge cutters or bale-makers. The tractor's engine is joined to these machines to make them work.

▶ Machinery like
this combine harvester
makes modern farming
very efficient.

Harvesters

Most farmers in rich countries own
tractors. They often hire the machines
they use for harvesting. Combine
harvesters cost a great deal of money.
Farmers need them only at harvest time.

A combine harvester does several
jobs. In the past, a team of people was
needed to do the same work. It would
take five people about a day to harvest
a hectare of wheat. A combine and its
driver can harvest 20 times as much
wheat in the same time.

Other machines

Tractors and combine harvesters are not
the only machines in farming. There are
large drying machines to dry the grain.
There are milking machines to milk the
cows. Farmers also use aircraft to spray
their fields. In Japan, they have machines
to plant out young rice plants in the
flooded paddies.

Farmers use computers, too. Today,
the farm records are often kept on a
computer. A computer can even work
out the right amount of food for a cow.

Raising animals

Hereford

Guernsey

Angus

Highland

Ankole

Khillari

Six different breeds of cattle from different parts of the world.

Farm animals are not just animals caught from the wild. Wild animals do not trust people. Farm animals are used to living with people. Their owners do not have to tame them, because they were born in captivity.

Many farm animals are raised for the food they give us. Chickens, for example, give us both eggs and meat. Cattle are kept for their meat and milk. The milk can be used to make butter and cheese. Other animals, like sheep, are also kept for their coats.

Which of these is the odd one out: dog, sheep, beaver, snail or cheetah? All of them except one have been used by people as tame, or **domestic**, animals. The dog is used for herding and hunting. The cheetah was once used for hunting as well. Sheep have been kept for their meat, milk and wool for about 6000 years. In Ancient Rome, people kept snails to eat. Nobody has tamed the beaver!

The cost of meat

Animals kept for meat need a lot to eat. They eat huge amounts of grass. They also eat food that has been grown for them, like barley. The farmer pays a lot of money for these foods. To get the money back, the meat has to sell for a high price.

Meat is an expensive food in another way. All the energy in food first comes from the sun. Then it passes to the plants. The animals take in the energy by eating the plants. They use a lot of the energy to keep warm and stay alive. Only a little goes to building up the meat in their bodies. So meat is a more wasteful food than plants, but many people still like to eat it.

Scottish blackface

Anglo-nubian (goat)

merino

▲ This picture shows a domestic pig and its ancestor, the wild boar.

What is breeding?

Farm animals often have mates chosen for them by their owners. Choosing mates like this is called **breeding**. Breeding is an important part of raising **livestock**. It is used to give people the types of animal they want. In Australia, farmers recently wanted a milking cow that could live in the hot climate. They mated European milking cows with the tough Indian zebu. This gave them a new breed.

When animals are mated, the owners hope that the young will be strong and healthy. Choosing two mates that are strong helps make sure that the young will be strong also.

Milk, butter and cheese

We keep some animals for the milk they make. The main ones are cows and goats. A cow cannot make milk until she has had a calf. Then she can give milk for 10 months.

A dairy farm

Most milk today comes from big herds of cows kept on **dairy** farms. The dairy farmer has grass fields for the cows to **graze** on. The fields are fed with fertilizer. In summer, some grass is cut and dried to make hay. The hay is given to the cows in the winter months, when they are inside.

The cows graze in the fields until it gets cold. Then they are kept indoors. During the winter, they live in big sheds and eat hay and other food.

Land, food and farm equipment are all costly. The farmer has to sell a lot of milk to make any money. The cows must be good milkers. A good milker can give more than 20 litres of milk a day.

camel

yak

reindeer

Friesian cow

Anglo-nubian goat

Racka sheep

All these animals provide milk for human beings.

The milking parlour

The cows have to be milked twice a day. The milking is done in a **milking parlour**. Each cow has a set of tubes fixed to her **udder**. The tubes connect to a machine which sucks the milk out. Then a truck called a tanker collects the milk and takes it to the dairy.

▲ Milking parlours must be clean and organized. The machines suck the milk out of the cows udders. Each cow produces about 45 litres of milk a day.

Many cows can be milked at once like this. They do not mind being milked by machine. They are often fed at the same time. Some farmers play music to the cows to keep them relaxed.

▼ Cheese being made in France. It is put into moulds and then left to ripen.

From milk to cheese

As soon as the milk arrives at the dairy, it is quickly heated, and then cooled. This stops it from going bad. Milk keeps longer when it is changed into milk **products**. Butter is a milk product. To make butter, the milk has to be stirred for a long time. This makes the fat stick together and become butter. To make cheese, things are added to milk to make it thicken. Then it is pressed together. Most cheeses are left for a long time before they are eaten.

Caring for animals

Caring for animals means giving them three main things. These are food, water and shelter.

Looking after livestock is hard work. It costs a lot of money. Some beef cattle need to eat 10 kg of grain to build up a single kilogram of meat. In the summer, a milking cow eats 70 kg of grass each day. In winter, cows need hay, **silage** and other plant feeds.

Farmers want to turn animal food into food for sale as soon as they can. They need the money to pay for wages and machines, as well as the animals' food.

Factory farm

There are two main ways of farming. On large farms, animals are left to move around in search of food. They hunt for food like grass. This is **extensive** farming. On **intensive** farms, the animals are kept together. They live and feed in a small space. Many farmers like to farm this way. They can raise many animals and sell them more cheaply.

▲ On a factory farm in Poland, the pigs are kept in stalls. They are given plenty of food.

▼ An intensive farm in Saudi Arabia. It is feeding time for the cattle.

Intensive farms are often called factory farms. Many pigs and calves are raised on factory farms. So are hens and turkeys. Most of the eggs and chicken we eat are from factory farms.

Factory farm animals cannot move about much. Some people say that factory farming is cruel. Others say that the animals are well looked after and are happy.

Sick animals

All farm animals have to be kept healthy. If cows are sick, they do not give as much milk. If meat animals are sick, they lose weight. So farmers always watch their animals for disease. They soon notice the first sign of illness in an animal.

Animals get diseases just like people do. Sometimes they give them to each other. Rinderpest is spread like this. It kills cattle in some parts of Africa. Some cattle in Africa also get another disease from an insect called the tsetse fly. The tsetse flies pass on the disease when they bite the cattle. Farmers can treat the disease with drugs, but many cattle still die.

Milking cows can get a disease in their udders. This spoils their milk. After a time, their milk dries up completely. It takes a long time to cure the cows. Farmers try to avoid the disease by keeping their milking parlours very clean. The milking machines are washed each time they are used.

▼ This vet in Pakistan is giving an injection to a lamb. It will protect it from disease.

Protecting the land

The number of people in the world gets bigger each year. More houses and roads are built. Cities grow larger. People look for new land to farm. They also try to grow more crops on the land they use already. In some places, the people overwork the land. All the goodness is taken from the soil. The land becomes useless.

The disappearing soil

The world's soil is like a thin skin covering the land. Soil is made of tiny bits of broken rock. This is mixed with rotted plants and animal remains. Soil takes a long time to form, but it can be ruined very quickly.

One way land can be harmed is by soil **erosion**. Erosion is the wearing away of the soil. Sometimes the wind can do this. In dry places, the soil dries to dust and is blown away.

Water erodes soil also. This makes farming on hills and slopes difficult. Heavy rain washes soil into the valleys. Then the streams and rivers pick up the soil and wash it downstream. Much of the soil ends up in the sea.

▲ Land can be washed away by water.
▼ The dry soil being stirred up by this tractor is being blown away by the wind.

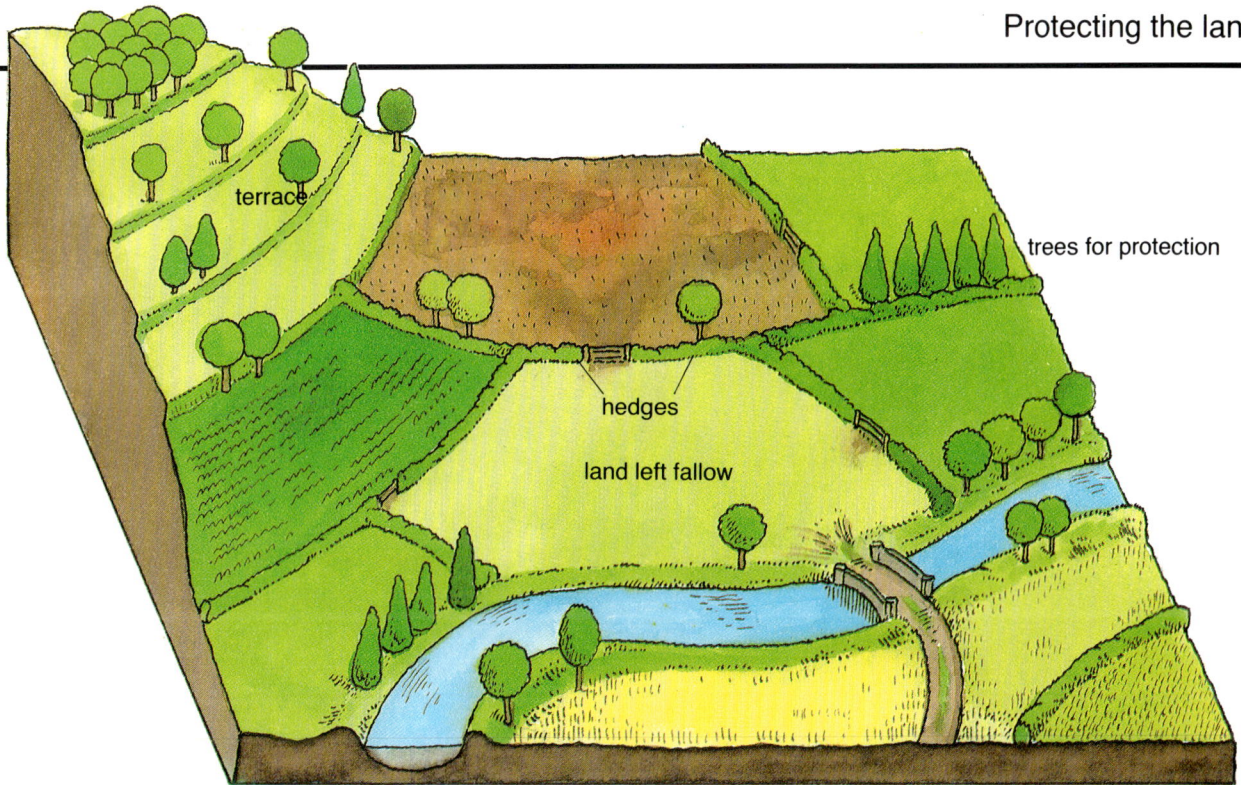

terrace

trees for protection

hedges

land left fallow

The human threat

Trees help to protect the land. The roots of trees hold the soil in place. The trees also hold a lot of water. In the past, there were many more trees. People cleared the trees and forests to make room for crops and animals. They used the wood to build houses and ships. Without the trees, the soil was no longer safe from high winds. There were less trees to soak up the rain. This made the low lands flood.

In many countries, too many trees are still cut down. Farmers need to grow as much as they can. The soil has to be fed with fertilizer to keep it rich. This is costly. In some countries, farmers do not have enough money to buy fertilizer. After a few years the soil becomes useless, and nothing can grow.

▲ Land can be used in many ways. It can be cut into terraces on hillsides. Hedges and trees can be grown to protect the land from wind. Some land can be left fallow for a year or two.

Rest and cure

When the land is damaged, it can take hundreds of years for new soil to be made. People now realize it is important to look after the land. One way of doing this is to let the ground rest. After growing a crop, it is left **fallow** for a year or two. Nothing is grown on it.

Trees and hedges are sometimes grown along the sides of fields. This protects the fields by slowing the winds down. On steep hillsides, people cut the land into steps, or **terraces**. Trees are also planted. Their roots keep the soil in place. The tree roots will stop the soil from being washed downhill.

Food from the sea

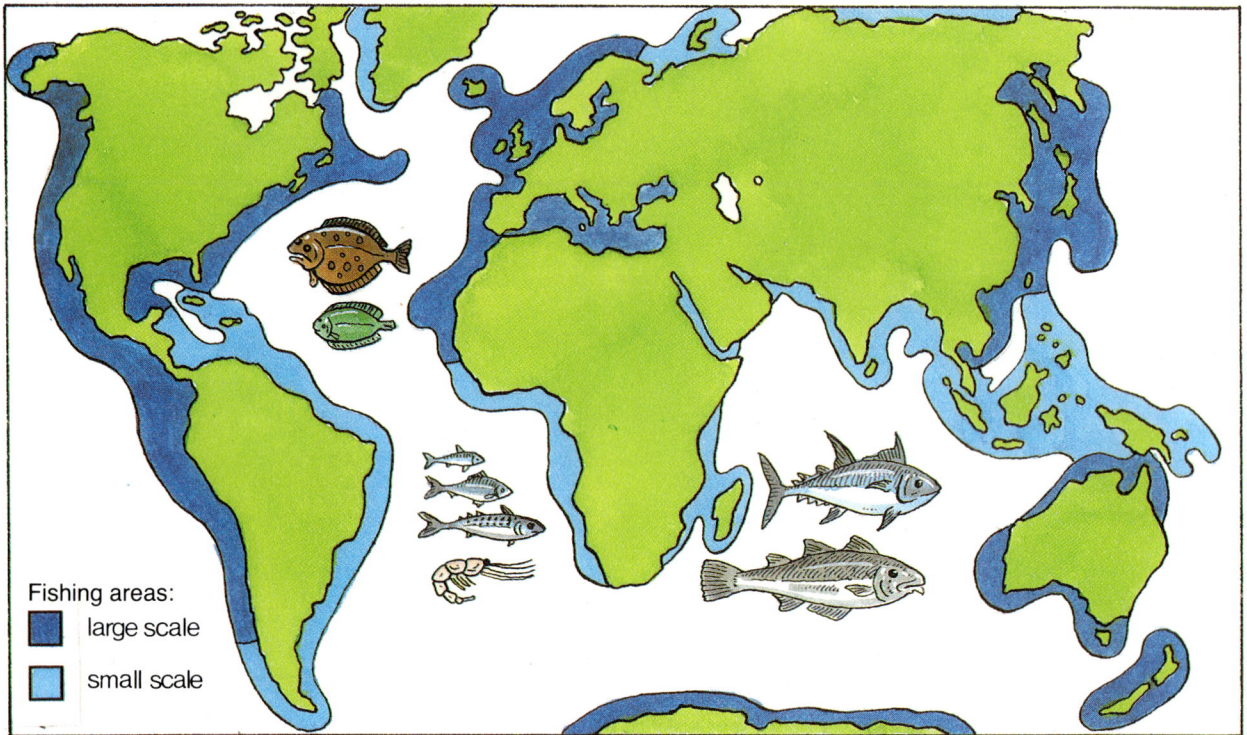

Fishing areas:
- large scale
- small scale

The seas and oceans cover more than two-thirds of the Earth. The sea is rich in food. We cannot farm the sea like dry land, but we can harvest it. In a few countries, such as Japan, people eat the plants which grow in the sea. But the most common type of seafood is fish.

Some parts of the sea have more fish in them than others. The North Atlantic is a good fishing ground. So is the west coast of North America. A lot of fish are caught near Japan and New Zealand.

Many fish eat tiny animals and plants called **plankton**. Plankton is very common in the cold seas of the world. Some of the world's best fishing grounds are near the Arctic and Antarctic regions where fish gather to feed.

Types of fish

Thousands of different animals live in the sea, but we only catch a few different types. Much of the seafood we catch is fed to farm animals. Two types of fish we often eat are cod and haddock. Many are caught off Newfoundland, in the North Atlantic. Two big ocean **currents** meet here and this makes it a good place for plankton. Cod and haddock swim near the bottom of the sea. Other types of fish, such as herring, tuna and mackerel, live near the surface.

Some sea animals do not swim at all. They have shells and fix themselves to rocks. Mussels are shellfish which do this. Other types of shellfish, like shrimps and crabs, do move around.

The fishing industry

Ocean fish are usually caught with large nets. This means huge numbers can be caught at the same time.

There are several types of not. One, like a giant bag, is called a trawl. The boat that tows the trawl is a trawler. The trawler drags the net behind it along the sea bed. As the net moves along, fish are trapped in it.

Many trawlers go to sea for weeks or even months at a time. They work far from land in all weathers. Deep-sea fishing can be dangerous. In storms, boats are sometimes sunk and their crews drowned.

Inshore fishing can be dangerous too. But inshore fishermen are away for only a night or so. They catch fish near the coasts. Modern ways of fishing work very well.

▼ A trawler hauling in a catch of fish.

More than 75 million tonnes of fish are caught in the world each year. Fish are very rich in protein. In Asia and Africa, about one-third of the protein eaten is in the form of fish. One-third of the world's total fish catch is used to feed animals.

▲ A Japanese fish market.

Storing and processing

Fresh food does not last for long. It dries up and loses some of its nutrients. Tiny organisms called **bacteria** start growing in it. This makes the food bad.

Many foods are only fresh once a year, when they are harvested. But food is needed all through the year. Food also has to be taken on long journeys to reach the shops. So we have to find ways to store the food we grow until we are ready to eat it.

Keeping food

People have always needed to store the food they grow. One of the oldest ways to store, or **preserve** food is to dry it. Grain keeps well in a dry place. Other crops, like peas and beans, can be kept fit to eat if they are dried before they are stored. Fish and meat also keep if they are dried.

Another way to keep food is to add salt to it. Meat and fish can be preserved

▲ An enormous warehouse where food is kept before despatch to stores and supermarkets.

with salt, and so can some vegetables like green beans. Sugar and vinegar preserve food, too. One way of keeping fruit is to make it into jam. Jam is made by adding sugar to fruit and heating it. Vegetables can be stored in vinegar to make pickles.

▲ In this canning factory, workers are sorting tomatoes. Some tomatoes will be peeled and canned. Others will be used for making tomato ketchup.

Canning and freezing

Today, people like to eat a wide range of foods. They also want food that takes less time to prepare.

A lot of scientists now study ways of keeping all the foods people want. Other experts work on ways of **packaging** them well.

Many types of food are sold in cans. Canned food can be kept for a year or more. It keeps because it is sealed in the can. No disease or bacteria can reach the food.

Another way of preserving food is by freezing it. Perhaps the best known frozen food is ice-cream. Deep-frozen food can be kept for weeks or months. Meat, fish, vegetables, fruit and dairy products can be frozen. Fish caught at sea are frozen as soon as they are caught in order to preserve them.

What are additives?

A lot of food we eat has passed through factories. If we look at the labels, they tell us what the factory has added to the food.

Some food contains chemicals to keep it from going bad. Fats, for example, can go bad. So a chemical is added to stop this happening. Colourings are also added to make the food look better. Other chemicals make the flavour stronger. Many people think that these additives can be harmful. They want to buy food without them.

Growing a surplus

More than half of the farmers in the world farm small plots of land. They grow only enough food for their families to eat. They have little left over to sell. This type of farming is called subsistence farming. The rest of the world's farmers grow food to sell. For them, farming is a business. They grow the crops which will fetch the best prices. The sale of the crops pays for machines and wages.

A lot of the food a country grows is eaten by its people. Some is sold to countries which grow different foods. All over the world, countries trade in food this way.

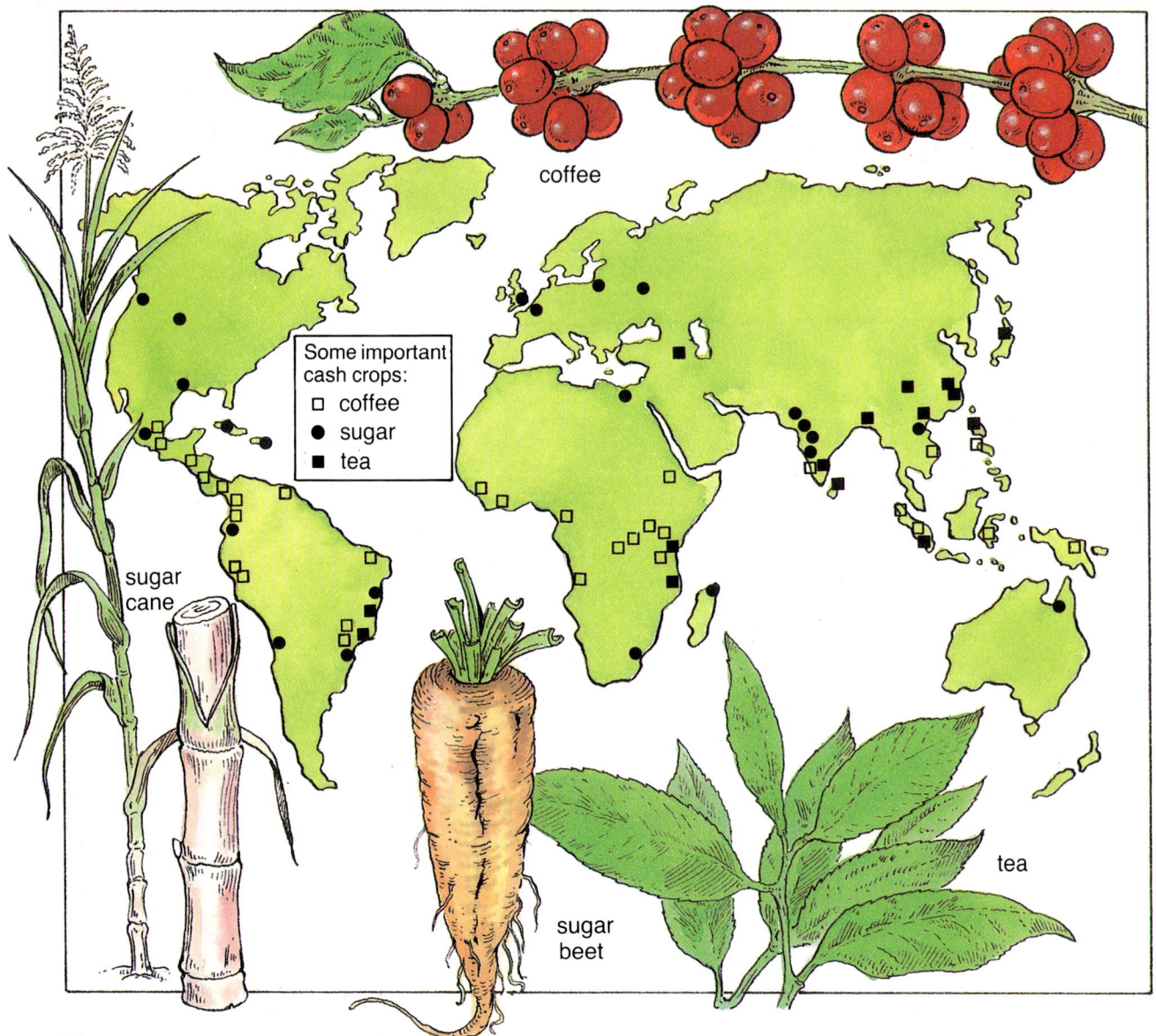

coffee

Some important cash crops:
- □ coffee
- ● sugar
- ■ tea

sugar cane

sugar beet

tea

▲ This picture shows wheat being unloaded from a ship's hold. The wheat has been exported from a country with a surplus.

Crops for cash

Different crops grow well in different places. Tea likes plenty of rain. It also needs to grow on hillsides where the water drains away quickly. Sugar needs a rich soil and a hot, damp climate. Coffee also likes heat and plenty of moisture. It likes growing in high places.

People all over the world like to drink tea and coffee. They also use a lot of sugar in food. So, in the countries where these crops do well, the farmers grow as much as they can. These crops are called cash crops. They are sold, or exported, all over the world. The farmers stop using their land to grow food to eat. The sales bring in a lot of money for their countries.

Growing too much

Today, people do not eat as much sugar as they used to. There is a glut on the world sugar market.

If there is too much of something, its price will come down. World sugar prices are now low. This is bad news for countries where the farmers grow a lot of sugar cane.

The same thing can happen to any country where a lot of one cash crop is grown. It helps if the farmers change to growing different crops. This is not always easy. The whole country may depend on selling the cash crops.

▼ This farmer in Trinidad has just started to harvest his coffee crop.

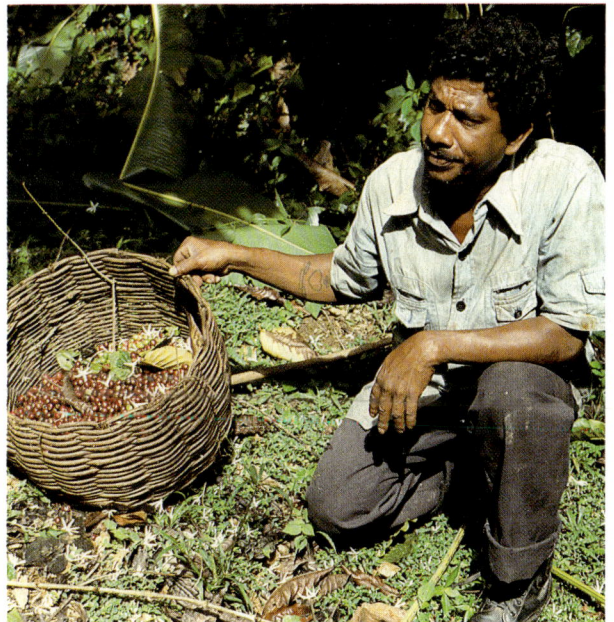

The farmer's year

Farmers need to plan their work for the year with care. They know how the weather changes with the seasons. They plan their year around the seasons. They are careful not to leave any jobs too late. If they left the sowing too late, for example, the crop might not have time to grow and ripen before the cold weather comes.

What to grow?

Each year, farmers have to choose which crops to grow. Their choice depends on several things. One of these is the weather. There is no point in growing maize in a cold, damp climate, or potatoes in a very dry one.

Farmers also have to work out which crops will sell. How will they get the crops to the market? Will they spoil on the way? Is their land suited to the crops they want to grow?

When the decisions are made, the farmer can set to work. The seed has to be bought, and the land ploughed.

Early in the year the seed is sown. Soon crops begin to grow. At different times, the young crops have to be sprayed or dusted with fertilizer.

When the crop is ripe, the harvesting begins. This is quickly done with a combine harvester. In some countries, there is time to grow a second crop.

Rice year

Wheat year

1

2

3

4

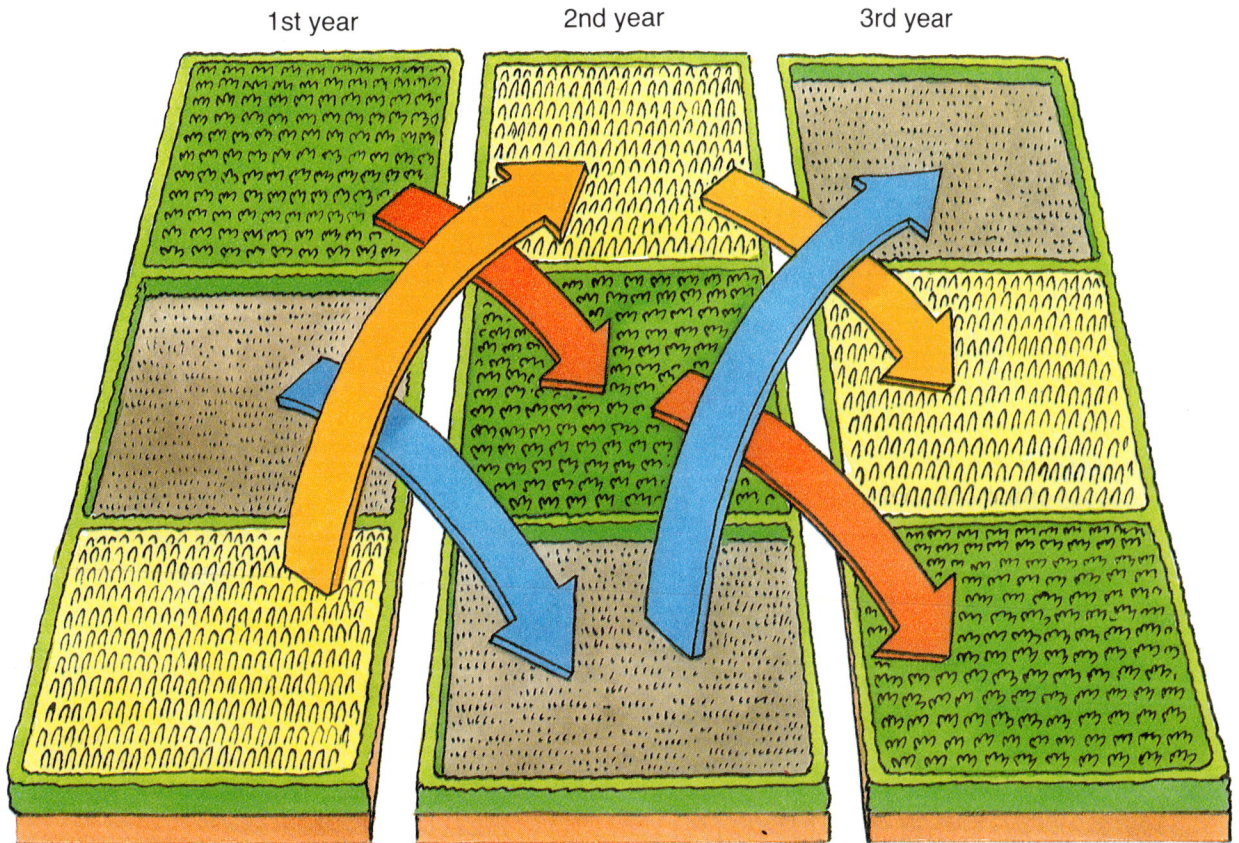

1st year   2nd year   3rd year

▲ Crop rotation is one way of using the land. The crops are varied from year to year to help the soil.

Good year or bad?

Farming is not an easy job. A lot can go wrong. The weather may be so wet that the crops are ruined. Another year it may be too dry. Frosts may spoil fruit blossom, so little fruit is formed. Insects may strip plants of their leaves or give diseases to a farmer's livestock. Laws may be passed which limit the amount of crops the farmer can grow. Such laws are passed to avoid too much of one food being grown. Many farmers can suffer as a result of this.

Crop rotation

The choice of crop depends on what the farmer has grown before. An old way of getting the most out of the land is called **crop rotation**. Each year, a different crop is grown in each field. A grain crop might be followed by a crop of beans. The roots of beans give nitrogen to the soil. So do those of clover and some other plants.

Once rice paddies are drained, rice can be rotated, too.

Growing our own food

Many people live in cities. Some people have gardens. Others live in apartments with balconies. Some have a patch that can be used as a small kitchen garden.

In the Far East, people in cities use every piece of earth they can find to grow food. They even grow food in big pots and tubs. City people everywhere can do the same. Those who have a bit of land bigger than a tub can grow bigger vegetables!

Growing our own food is fun. The food tastes good. We know it is fresh when we eat it. We learn what farming is about — even if our farm is only one square metre in size!

SOME KITCHEN GARDENS AROUND THE WORLD

United Kingdom

POTATOES grow well in the U.K.'s damp climate. Potato plants grow from seed potatoes. After planting, they take about four months to grow. Potatoes need a lot of room to grow.

Most people eat BROAD BEANS without their pods. If they are picked when they are very young, the pods can be eaten too.

SPRING ONIONS are harvested before their white bulbs swell. More should be sown every three weeks.

LETTUCES can be grown all year but producing crops for winter and early spring is not easy. They grow best in the summer months.

United States

PUMPKINS are a famous American vegetable. They can grow to an enormous size. People make them into soup and pies.

TOMATOES are grown all over the United States. They like warm weather. Some have fruits that weigh almost one kilo.

COLLARDS taste like cabbage. They can grow in very cold climates.

SNOW PEAS are also called 'mangetout'. This is French for 'eat it all' — the pods as well! They were bred to do well in hot, dry weather.

A large pumpkin!

In 1984, a pumpkin weighing nearly 200 kg was grown in England at Stockbridge, Hampshire.

Far East

LEI-CHOI are Chinese greens. They have thick leaves and fat, crisp stems. They start trying to flower and grow seeds before the weather gets too cold

CUCUMBERS can be grown up canes, like a vine. One of the longest types of cucumber is called Kyoto, after a city in Japan.

ASIAN RADISHES are different from western ones. The Asian ones are long and white.

GARLIC is easy to grow. Buy a bulb, break off the cloves, and plant them in a sunny spot.

Africa

MAIZE grown in Africa is often ground into flour. The cobs are also boiled and roasted.

OKRA is a bushy plant with yellow flowers and long green seed pods. In English, okra is called 'Ladies' Fingers'.

PEANUTS or groundnuts are very nutritious. They like plenty of warmth and rain.

YAM is a root crop. Yams contain plenty of carbohydrate. Some grow very large.

BANANAS The green banana or plantain is a staple diet in East Africa.

CASSAVA roots are pounded up and made into flour for making bread.

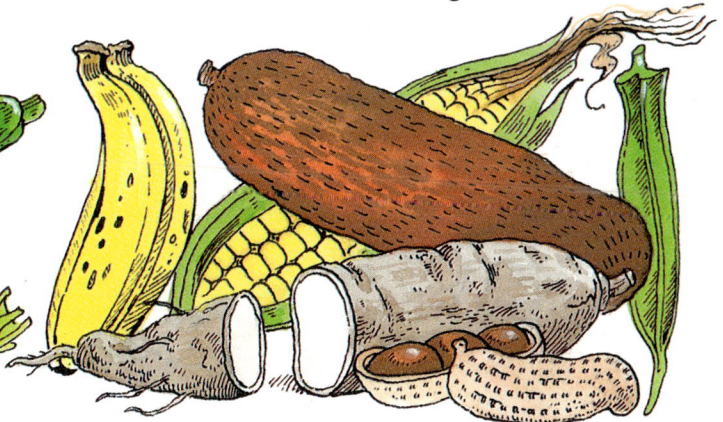

Food for survival

Crops can fail for many reasons. If the land floods, the crops are ruined. If there is no rain at all, they dry up and die. The people and animals who depend on the crops have nothing to eat. They can die from lack of food. Many thousands of people have died in the **droughts** that started in Africa in the early 1980s.

Pests can also ruin a crop. A large swarm of locusts can strip a field bare. Other insects and rats can do great damage to harvests in store.

Countries can guard against crop failure by building up stores of food. Rich countries have big stores. Poor countries do not have enough food left over to make large stores.

▲ A failed crop of sunflowers on a farm in Kenya. The plants died because there was not enough rain.

The desert locust

One desert locust can eat its own weight, about two grams, of food in one day.

There can be as many as 40 000 million locusts in one large swarm. If each locust eats its own weight of food the swarm can destroy 80 million kg of food in one day.

This is enough food to feed 400 000 people for a whole year.

Countries in need

In recent years, many countries have suffered from **famine**. In 1984, for example, 21 African countries were very short of food. There had been drought and war. This brought famine to 150 million people.

People in other countries were in trouble as well. Many of them lived in parts of South America and Asia.

Drought and wars are not the only reasons for famine. In some cases, the people are just too poor to buy food. In these countries, transport is often bad. This makes it hard to move food to where it is needed.

▼ Famines are caused by floods as well as by droughts. Floods like this one in Bolivia can damage the land and spoil the crops.

▲ Food aid being handed out to hungry people in Ethiopia during the famine in 1984.

Food aid

Huge amounts of money and aid have been given to help starving people in Africa and other countries. The food this money buys is saving the lives of millions of people, but there are still problems.

It is not always easy to send the food to where it is needed. Niger is one country in Africa which is short of food. Food aid to Niger is sent to the nearest port. This is Cotonou, 1000 km from the country's border. The food aid is needed another 1000 km into the country. In all, the food has to travel 2000 km by road.

The road is often in bad repair. A flood may have torn away a bridge, or a truck may break down. There may be no spare parts for the trucks. The food will take a long time to reach the place where it is needed.

Experts believe that food stores should be set up all over Africa. If crops fail in the future, food aid would be close by.

Food for the future

Each year, the number of people in the world rises. In 1984, the world's population was about 4500 million people. A year later it had risen by 80 million. More food is needed each year to feed all the people in the world.

There is plenty of food in the world, but a lot of it is in the wrong place. The rich countries have two-thirds of the world's store of cereals. However, only one-third of the people in the world live in these countries.

To feed all the people in the world — rich and poor — we have to find better ways of farming.

▼ These tomatoes are being grown without soil. This way of growing food is called hydroponics.

▲ This scientist is looking at new ways of growing cereal crops.

New plant foods

Many scientists are looking at ways to make better use of the land. They tell farmers which crops will grow best in their soil. Plant breeders are finding new crops to suit all types of soil and climate. The Yeheb bush, for instance, grows well in very hot, dry places. The seeds of this bush can be used for food in desert lands.

Research into new crops is going on all over the world. Usually, soya beans do well only in fairly cool climates. The types grown in the tropics do not do well. Now, breeders in Africa have **crossbred** the two types. They now have beans that do well in hot climates.

In Taiwan, breeders have grown giant tomatoes. They are nearly four times as big as they used to be.

Pests and disease

Other people look at ways of protecting crops against pests and diseases. Plants which resist disease are being bred. Animals which eat pests are being used to kill the pests. This is an old idea. People use cats to catch mice! Insects are now used to catch other insects. Wasps are used to protect cassava crops from the mealybugs that eat them. The wasps eat the bugs.

Insects work against weeds, too. In Australia, they are used to kill a cactus that has become a nuisance.

▼ This picture shows three plants which could provide food in the future. Some are able to grow on poor soil, whatever the climate.

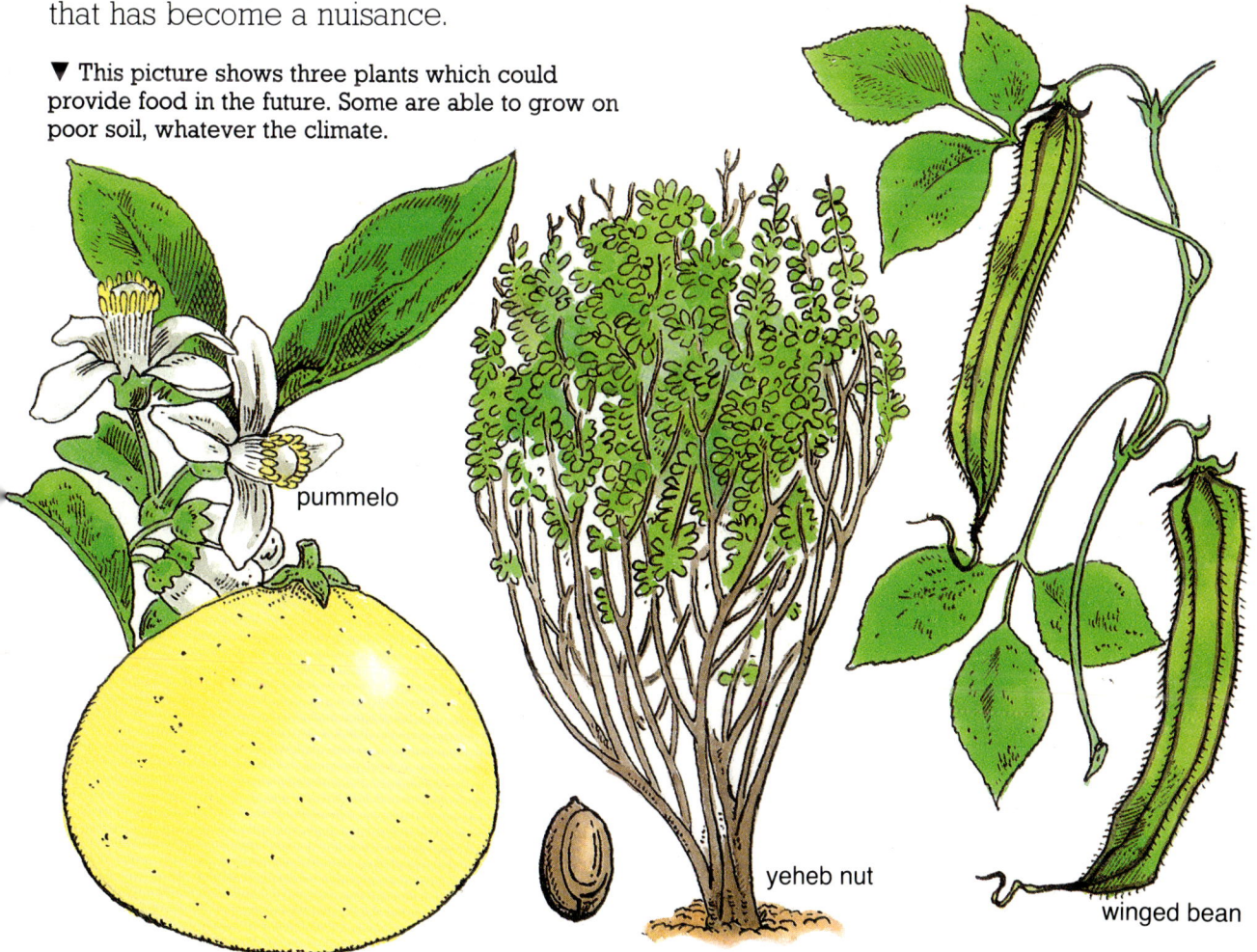

What will we eat?

Some scientists are working on new types of food. Not long ago, soya bean 'meat' was a new food. Now many people eat it.

Seaweed is another source of food that could be used much more. Research is also being done on tiny water plants called **algae**. They might soon be used for food as well. So might the plankton in the sea.

pummelo

yeheb nut

winged bean

Farming and science

Farming is hard work. It is also a science. Farmers work with the help of many types of scientist.

One of the jobs of a scientist is to observe and understand things about nature. This helps them to work out better ways of doing things. The first people to use crop rotation were doing this. They were working out better ways to farm. The people who bred better livestock were doing the same thing. The people who make new machines are engineers. Engineers have a big part to play in the science of farming.

Biologists study how living things work. They also help farmers. So do the scientists who study the weather. Chemists work on ways of making the best fertilizers.

Some of this work is done in factories. Some is done in colleges where research goes on. A lot of research is done on the farms themselves.

What we eat in the future depends a lot on science. It also depends on governments in different parts of the world. They can decide what is to be done about food for the world

▼ Growing crops in glasshouses calls for a wide range of scientific skills.

Glossary

algae: simple plants, without proper roots, stems or leaves

bacteria: minute living things, some of which may cause disease

breeding: the producing of young animals by choosing which adult animals mate with each other

carbohydrate: any substance made up of carbon, hydrogen and oxygen. The starch and sugar made by plants are carbohydrates

carbon dioxide: one of the gases in air. It is made up of carbon and oxygen. It has no colour or smell

cereal: a grain used for food. Rice, wheat, oats and barley are cereals

chemical: any substance which may change when it is joined or mixed with another substance

chlorophyll: the green substance in plants. Plants need chlorophyll to make their food

climate: the usual weather in a part of the world throughout the year

combine harvester: a moving machine that harvests a crop and separates out the grain

crop rotation: the planting of different crops in a field each year. This helps to keep the land fertile. If one type of plant is grown only, the soil loses its goodness

crossbreed: to produce a plant (or animal) by breeding from two different types

current: a flow of water in an ocean or river

dairy: describes a type of farm on which animals are kept for their milk

diet: the mixture of foods and amount that a person eats

domestic: describes an animal that is tame and looked after by people

drought: a long, dry period of weather, with little or no rain

energy: the power to do work

erosion: the wearing away of the soil by the action of the wind or the rain

extensive: describes a type of farming where animals are left to graze over a wide area

fallow: land which has no crops growing on it for a year or more

famine: a serious shortage of food. It causes starvation. Famines usually take place because of a disaster like a bad drought

fat: an important food, with a high energy content. Fat is found is animal tissue and plant seeds, e.g. fish liver, olives, peanuts and butter

fertile: soil that is rich and suitable for growing plants

fertilizer: any substance which is added to the soil to make plants grow better

fungus: any one of a large group of simple plants which includes yeasts, moulds, rusts and mushrooms

graze: to feed on grass. Cows and sheep are grazing animals

harvest: to gather crops when they are ripe

harvester: a machine which cuts and gathers a crop

inshore: carried on near the shore

intensive: describes a type of farming where as much food as possible is produced from a small area of land. This normally means buying in animal feed or plant fertilizer

livestock: animals kept on a farm

milking parlour: a special building in which cows are milked

mineral: any natural material found in the ground. Iron, salt and stone are minerals

nutrient: any substance that is nourishing or provides food. Nutrients keep the body healthy

organic: describes any material which contains carbon. Carbon is found in all living things

oxygen: a gas that is part of air and water. Oxygen has no colour, taste or smell. We need it to stay alive

packaging: the packing of something so that it can be stored and transported without being spoilt. The packaging is made as attractive as possible to help sell the item

photosynthesis: in green plants, the making of soluble plant foods from carbon dioxide and water, using the energy from sunlight

plankton: tiny plants and animals that float near the surface of the sea and freshwater lakes. Plankton is a source of food for many water animals

preserve: to keep something so that it does not spoil, or change

product: something that has been made, or produced. Butter is a product of milk

protein: one of a number of substances which are needed for the life and growth of all living things. Proteins are found in foods such as meat, fish, eggs and milk

pulse: the edible seeds of peas, beans and other pod-bearing plants

root crop: a type of crop, the roots of which are eaten as food. Carrots and turnips are root crops

seed: the part of a plant that will grow into a new plant, given the right conditions

silage: cut grass or other plants which are stored as winter food for cattle

staple food: a food that forms the main part of a diet. Rice is a staple food

starch: a white substance with no taste or smell, found in grain and many root crops. Starch is a carbohydrate

terrace: a flat, level area cut from a slope

transport: to carry goods (or people) from one place to another

tuber: a swollen underground root that stores food. A potato is a tuber

udder: the bag-like, milk-producing organ of certain female animals, such as cows, sheep and goats

vegetable: a plant that is grown for food, other than a fruit

vegetarian: a person who does not eat meat, fish or eggs, but eats only plant foods

vitamin: one of a number of substances, found in food, that are needed in small amounts by animals to keep them healthy

yield: anything that is given out or produced